Chinese Tale Series

中 国 神 话 故 事

The Cowherd and the Girl Weaver

牛 郎 织 女

Adapted by Chu Yi
Translated by Liu Guangdi
Illustrated by Wang Weizhi
改编　初　旖
翻译　刘光第
绘画　王味之

DOLPHIN BOOKS
海 豚 出 版 社

First Edition 2005

ISBN 978-7-80138-559-8

Published by Dolphin Books
24 Baiwanzhuang Road, Beijing 100037,China

Printed in the People's Republic of China

On the summer night with an breeze blowing lightly, on the banks of the Milky Way in the sky, there are two brightest stars, just like a pair of sweethearts looking at each other across the river. The star on the farther bank of the Milky Way was called Vega (It is called "Star of the Girl Weaver" in China), named after the fairy maiden called "the Girl Weaver". She is the most beautiful and clever daughter of God and the West Queen Mother. The one on the nearer bank of the Milky Way is called Altar (in Chinese, it is called "Star of the Cowherd"), derived from the industrious and good-natured cowherd; the two small stars on the two sides of it are their children.

晚风吹拂的夏夜，在天上的银河两岸，有两颗最耀眼的星星，好像两个期待相会的恋人，隔河相望。银河对岸的那颗叫织女星，是天上的天帝和王母最漂亮、聪慧的女儿织女仙子化成的。银河的这边是勤劳、善良的牛郎化作的，在他的左右各有一颗小星星，是他们的一对儿女。

相传，在远古的时候，天与地之间仅隔了一条天河。因为河水清澈，常引得天上的仙女们到天河沐浴。而凡人却看不到天河那边仙界，也不敢到天河里来，因为只要人进来，就会永远地消失了。

In the ancient times, heaven and earth were not so far apart as now, being separated by only one heavenly river. There was clear running water in the river, which often attracted the celestial fairies to bathe here. But common people could not see the celestial world beyond the Heavenly River, nor dared they enter the river, for all those who had entered it had never returned.

God and the West Queen Mother had the supreme power in the two worlds. The West Queen Mother often rode her dragon cart to visit the places on the banks of the Heavenly River.

天帝和王母拥有两个世界的最高权力。王母常常驾着龙车巡视天河两岸。

They had a daughter called "Girl Weaver", with pink tender skin as smooth as silk, and fine hair like a black waterfall. She was not only pretty, but also diligent, intelligent, and very kindhearted.

他们有个十七岁的女儿，叫织女，肌肤粉嫩、光滑如脂，乌黑的秀发就像黑色的瀑布。她不仅漂亮，而且勤劳、聪慧，心地非常善良。

After weaving the cloud brocade and heavenly clothing every day, Girl Weaver would fly together with her fairy sisters to the Heavenly River for bathing. She yearned for the earthly life, but the heavenly law did not allow her to cross the Heavenly River freely.

织女仙子每天织完了云锦天衣，就和姐妹们一起在傍晚时飞到天河中沐浴。她非常向往人间的生活，但是天规不允许她擅自越过天河。

Girl Weaver fell in love with a boy in the human world who was about the same age as her. He got up early to work at sunrise and returned late at sunset. His name was Cowherd, with parents dead, only living with an old buffalo as his good companion.

His life was very hard, but Cowherd felt he was very free and happy. Sometimes, he could not help singing a joyful song. When Girl Weaver heard such a joyful sound, her mood became happy too. But Cowherd did not know a fairy see him every day and love him so deeply.

织女仙子爱上了一个年纪与她相仿的人间男子，他日出而作、日没而息，非常勤劳。他的名字叫牛郎，无父无母，只与一头老水牛相依为命。日子虽然艰苦，但是牛郎感到自己很自由、也很快乐，有时，他会情不自禁地唱起欢快的歌儿。织女听到这快乐的歌声，心里也快乐起来了。

但牛郎并不知道有个日日与他相见的天上仙女深深地爱着他。

Whenever Girl Weaver saw Cowherd walking along the Heavenly River every day, she would be reluctant to leave, yet, she could do nothing but sign helplessly.

织女仙子每天依恋地看着牛郎从天河走过，只能无奈地叹息。

The old buffalo living together with Cowherd was a treasure inherited from his ancestors. As it had eaten the godly grass called "glossy ganoderma" grown at the high mountains, it had acquired the intelligence of a god. It could see each and every move of the fairy Girl Weaver in the celestial world, and it told all it had seen to Cowherd.

跟随牛郎的老水牛是牛郎的祖辈传下来的，因为吃了高山灵芝，具有神的灵性。它能看到仙界织女仙子的一举一动，就把这些都告诉了牛郎。

Cowherd was attracted deeply by such a lovely girl. The old buffalo gave Cowherd several cucumber seeds and told him to sow them and put up some cucumber trellises near the Heavenly River.

听老牛说完，牛郎也深深地被这个可爱的女孩儿吸引了。老水牛给了牛郎几粒黄瓜子，嘱咐他在天河边上搭架种下。

By the evening of the next day, the seeds sown on the previous day had grown into cucumbers hanging all over the trellises. Following the old buffalo's suggestion, Cowherd hid himself under the cucumber trellises as early as he could.
The miracle occurred: Cowherd was able to see the celestial world beyond the Heavenly River! When the fairies flew to the Heavenly River and hung their clothes on a glazed tree on the other bank, Cowherd recognized the Girl Weaver mentioned by the old buffalo at first sight.

第二天傍晚，前一天种下的瓜子已黄瓜满架。牛郎依老牛所说的，早早地躲在了黄瓜架下。

奇迹发生了，牛郎居然能够看到天河那边的仙界！当仙女们又飞到天河，将衣服挂在对岸一棵琉璃树上的时候，牛郎一眼就认出了老牛说的织女仙子。

Girl Weaver also noticed the Cowherd hidden under the cucumber trellises immediately. While the sisters were absorbed in their bathing and playing, they two ogled at each other silently.

织女仙子也一眼就看见了藏在黄瓜架下的牛郎。趁着姐妹们沐浴嬉戏的时候，两人默默地凝视着对方。

It was time to return to the court of Heaven. Urged by the other fairies, Girl Weaver had to leave the Heavenly River and Cowherd with great reluctance.

回天庭的时刻到了，在众仙女的催促下，织女万般无奈地离开了天河，离开了牛郎。

In a trance, Cowherd was gazing at the Heavenly River that had become vacant suddenly, and crying out the name of Girl Weaver. How he wished Girl Weaver to stay with him forever!

牛郎失神地望着突然空旷的天河，无奈地大声呼喊着织女仙子的名字，他多想让织女永远留在眼前呀！

The next evening, the fairies came to the Heavenly River for merriment again. Riding the old buffalo, Cowherd reached the glazed tree on the other bank of the Heavenly River, and took away the green dress of Girl Weaver from the glazed tree. Without dress, the fairy Girl Weaver would be unable to fly back.

第二天黄昏，仙女们又来到天河嬉戏，老水牛载牛郎到天河中的琉璃树下，取下了织女仙子的绿衣，没有这件衣服，织女仙子就不能飞回去了。

The old buffalo asked Cowherd to return the dress on the cucumber trellises, and then hide up. All the fairies flew back to the court of Heaven except Girl Weaver. She went under the cucumber trellises to meet him.

老水牛又让牛郎把衣服挂在黄瓜架上，然后躲起来。

众仙女都回天庭了，织女留了下来，到黄瓜架下与牛郎相会。

Cowherd and Girl Weaver found each other congenial and full of mutual affection. Hand in hand happily, together with the old buffalo, they went home, singing all the way.

牛郎和织女仙子情投意合、两心相悦，幸福地手牵着手，与老水牛一起回家了，快乐的牛郎把山歌洒了一路。

Cowherd and Girl Weaver got married as they had wished. Girl Weaver introduced the celestial weaving technology to the human world, and people learned how to raise silkworm and make silk clothes. The human world became as flourishing as the celestial world.

Cowherd and Girl Weaver were both diligent and intelligent. He tilled the land while she weaved cloth. They lived a very happy life, and everyone praised them.

牛郎和织女仙子如愿地成为恩爱的夫妻。织女仙子将天上的纺织技术带到人间，从此人们便会养蚕织锦，人间也有了仙界的繁华。

牛郎、织女两人勤劳聪慧，男耕女织，小日子过得和和美美，人见人夸。

One year later, they had a pair of children: the boy was called "Jinger" (Gold Brother), and the girl was called "Yumeir" (Jade Sister). The two children were grown up, which made their happy life even happier.

一年后，他们生了一双儿女，男孩儿叫金哥儿，女孩儿叫玉妹，两个孩子渐渐长大，更给他们增添了无穷的欢乐。

One day, the heavenly generals Qianliyan (Clairvoyance) and Shunfeng'er (Clairaudient) found that Girl Weaver had secretly descended to the human world and married Cowherd, and reported it to the West Queen Mother. She flew into a rage at the news, and immediately ordered the heavenly generals to catch Girl Weaver back to the court of Heaven for punishment.

一天，天将千里眼和顺风耳发现织女私自下凡与牛郎结为夫妻，就将此事报告了王母。王母听后勃然大怒，命令天将把织女仙子捉回天庭问罪。

One day, when the sun had just risen, Cowherd said good-bye to his wife quite early as usual, driving his old buffalo to the field to do his farm work. After finishing her housework, Girl Weaver began to play with their children Jinger and Yumeir.

All of a sudden, up came a great thunderclap in the clear sky, black clouds gathered overhead, accompanied by thundering and lightning, and the heavenly army caught Girl Weaver and took her away, leaving the two crying children.

这天太阳刚刚升起，牛郎还像往常一样早早地与妻儿道别，赶着老水牛一起耕田去了。织女仙子做完家务，就陪金哥儿和玉妹玩了起来。

突然间，晴空打了一个巨大的霹雳，刹那间乌云密布、电闪雷鸣，天将捉走了织女仙子，全然不顾两个哭泣的孩子。

Cowherd was shocked at the changing weather. The old buffalo knew Girl Weaver had already been taken away by the West Queen Mother, so it said to Cowherd, "Cowherd, I have lived for four hundred years, and I am dying now. After death, I will become a manteau and a pair of shoes. Put them on, and then you will be able to fly to Heaven. Your wife has been caught and taken away by the West Queen Mother. Hurry up, chase them!"

牛郎看到如此反常的天象，惊诧不已。老水牛知道织女仙子已被王母派人捉走，就对牛郎说："牛郎呀，我已经活了四百岁了，我要死了，我死之后会变作一件披风和一双鞋子，你穿上它就可以上天了。你的妻子被王母捉走了，你快去追吧！"

The old buffalo changed itself into a manteau and a pair of shoes. Cowherd put them on and flew home. He found his two children crying.

老牛说完就化作一件披风和一双鞋子，牛郎穿上后飞奔回家，两个孩子正在啼哭。

Because Girl Weaver descended to the human world and married Cowherd without permission, the West Queen Mother was extremely angry, so she came and took Girl Weaver back herself. Shortly after crossing the Heavenly River, they saw Cowherd following them from far away, carrying his children in two baskets.

因为织女私自下凡与与郎成亲，王母特别恼怒，亲自来押织女，刚过天河，远远地就见牛郎担着儿女追了过来。

Wearing the shoes and manteau derived from the old buffalo, Cowherd flew very fast, and soon he was near to Girl Weaver, separated only by a river. Suddenly the West Queen Mother turned around and took out her godly hairpin. She made a wave of it, pointing to the Heavenly River and murmuring some incantation.

牛郎穿着老牛变成的鞋子和披风飞得很快，眼看与织女只有一河之隔，王母突然转身，从头上拔出神簪念动咒语，对准天河划去。

Immediately, the clear and shallow Heavenly River moved up, far away from the earth, raising thousands of waves, which separated Girl Weaver from Cowherd. The two shouted to each other fretfully, across the surging Heavenly River. Cowherd and Girl Weaver, were separated by the ruthless Heavenly River.

刹那间，昔日清且浅的天河忽然远离大地，掀起千层波浪将织女与牛郎分开。两个人隔着汹涌澎湃的天河焦急地呼喊。深深相爱着的牛郎和织女，被无情的天河分开。

The West Queen Mother hated Girl Weaver deeply for her bold violation of the heavenly law and regulations, so she decided to punish her severely. She ordered that Girl Weaver should never see Cowherd again, otherwise, she would get the harshest punishment from the court of Heaven. Girl Weaver would rather die than yield to the West Queen Mother. The West Queen Mother was very angry.

王母深恨织女擅自违反天规天条，决定严惩织女。她命令织女永远不再见牛郎，否则，将受到天界最严厉的惩罚。织女誓死不肯屈从，王母非常恼怒。

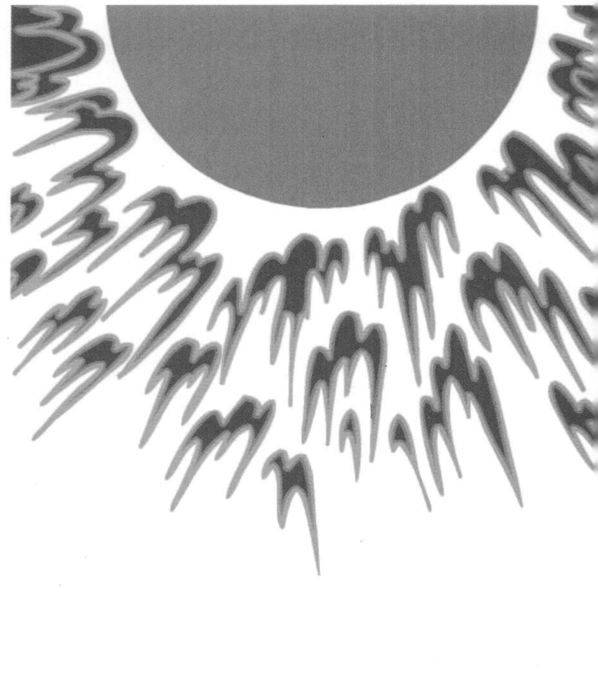

At first, Girl Weaver was locked in the eternal iceberg, but she did not yield. Then, she was put on the sun table, suffering from all kinds of torture,but she still refused to give in. She missed Cowherd and her two children day and night, and wept until she had almost no tears to shed.

织女先被锁在万年冰山之中，不屈服；又被投在太阳台上，受尽了折磨，但她仍不屈服。她日夜思念牛郎和一双儿女，眼泪都快哭干了。

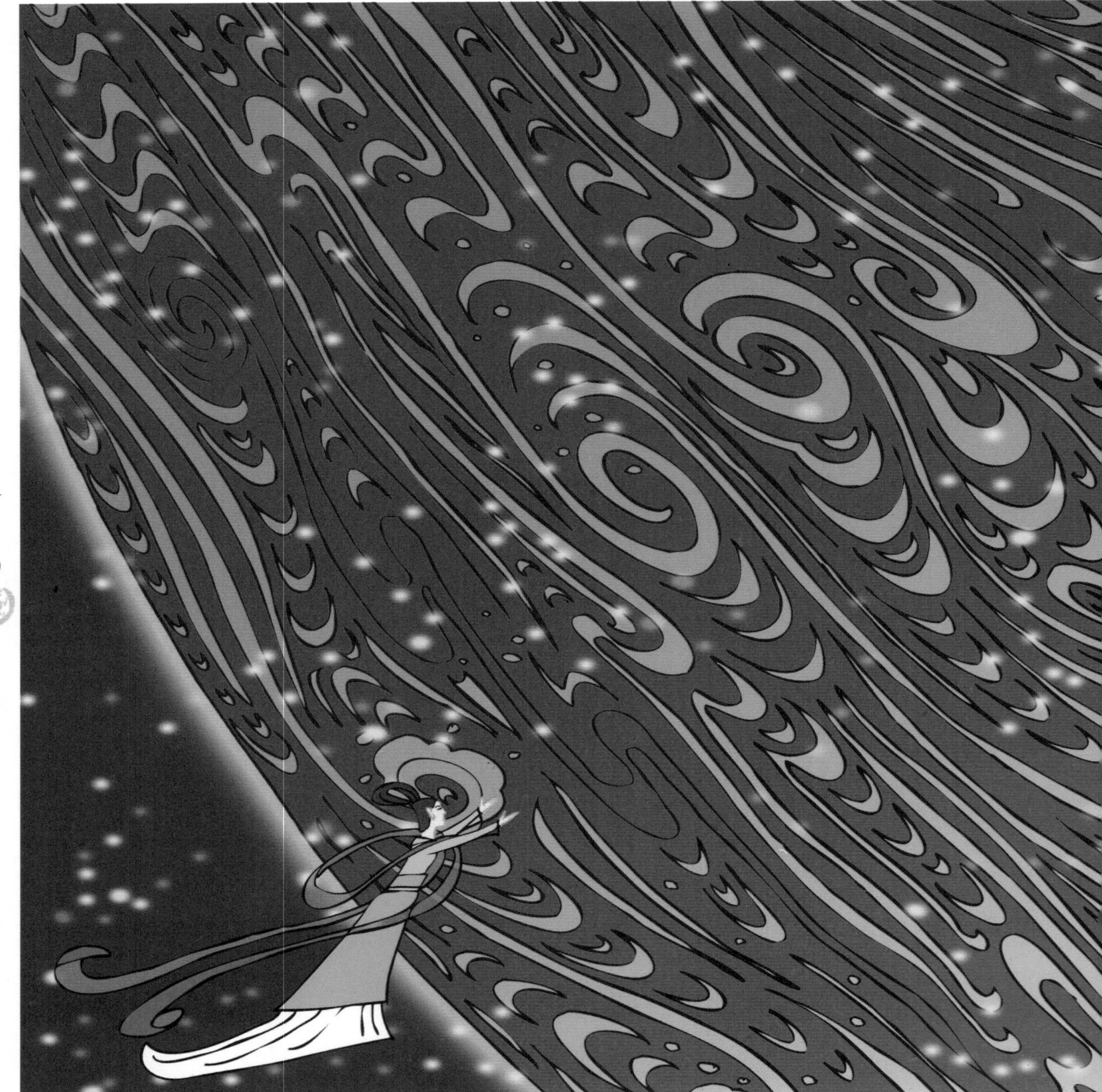

Girl Weaver yearned for her husband and children, while Cowherd yearned for his wife,and their children cried all day long, shouting for their mom. When the West Queen Mother found her daughter getting gaunt increasingly , her heart softened, too. Finally, she decided to allow them to meet across the Heavenly River on July 7th once every year.

织女思念着丈夫和孩子，牛郎思念着妻子，孩子整天哭着喊着要妈妈。王母娘娘看着日渐憔悴的女儿，也心软了，最后，王母决定，准许他们每年的七月七日在天河边隔河见一次面。

On the banks of the vast Milky Way in the sky, they looked at each other affectionately from afar. Magpies were moved by their steadfast love, so, on July 7th of the lunar calendar, all magpies would fly to the Heavenly River voluntarily without prior consultation.

浩瀚的天上银河两岸，他们深情地遥遥相望。喜鹊们都被他们忠贞的爱情感动了，在这一年的七月初七日，所有的喜鹊都不约而同地飞到天河。

The magpies gathered together to form a magpie bridge linking one side of the Heavenly River with the other side for Cowherd and Girl Weaver, so the couple could meet again .

July 7th of Chinese lunar calendar is the day when Cowherd and Girl Weaver meet, and is also a day for all lovers in the world to meet.

喜鹊们都聚到一起，从天河的这边到天河的那边，为牛郎和织女仙子架起一座鹊桥，相爱的人终于又可以相会了。

中国历每年的七月初七日，是天上的牛郎和织女仙子相会的日子，也是凡间的情人们相会的日子。

图书在版编目（CIP）数据

牛郎织女 / 初旖改编；王味之绘；刘光第译.
北京：海豚出版社，2005.10
(中国神话故事)
ISBN 978-7-80138-559-8

I. 牛… II. ①初… ②王… ③刘… III. 图画故
事—中国—当代—英汉 IV. I287.8

中国版本图书馆 CIP 数据核字（2005）第 115078 号

中国神话故事
牛郎织女

改编：初 旖
绘画：王味之
翻译：刘光第
社址：北京百万庄大街 24 号 邮编：100037
印刷：北京地大彩印厂
开本：16 开（787 毫米 × 1092 毫米）
文种：英汉 印张：3
版次：2005 年 10 月第 1 版 2010 年 1 月第 4 次印刷
标准书号：ISBN 978-7-80138-559-8
定价：15.00 元